When
BASILDON
was farms and fields

JESSIE K. PAYNE

IAN HENRY PUBLICATIONS

The illustration on the cover
is of Merricks Farm, Vange,
from a watercolour by H Thompson, c.1900

British Library Cataloguing in Publication Data

Payne, Jessie K.
  When Basildon was farms and fields.
  1. Basildon (Essex)——History
  I. Title
  942.6'772   DA690.B28

  ISBN 0-86025-416-X

Printed for
Ian Henry Publications, Ltd.
20 Park Drive, Romford, Essex RM1 4LH
by
Booksprint, 1a Marsh Lane, Ashton, Bristol BS3 2NR

CONTENTS

Most of these articles originally appeared in
the Basildon Standard
who have graciously given permission
to republish them

Of the men who lived in the forests and fens of prehistoric Basildon few traces have been found, but there is one relic left by a prehistoric hunter of deer, wild boar, wild ox or wolves to be seen in Billericay's Cater Museum - a sling-stone found in 1960 near the Duke's Head on Laindon Common.

One of the earliest implements found in Basildon is at Prittlewell Priory Museum, Southend. It is a fine specimen of a stone hammer or mace head that a late Neolithic (New Stone Age) or early Bronze Age man probably lost at what is now the junction of Whitmore Way and Timberlog Lane.

In the later years of the 19th century a fine Bronze Age celt or axe-like implement was found on Merricks Marsh, near Marsh Farm, on the south side of the Fenchurch Street railway line at Vange. It was found six feet below the surface when some brick-making machinery was installed.

Another interesting discovery was four feet below ground when Swan Mead School was being built on the corner of Bull Road and Church Road. This was a bronze founder's hoard of about sixty or seventy bronze pieces. The spot seems to have been the workshop of a man who made implements for a settlement in a clearing of the forest and it is believed to date between 1000 and 750 BC, when members of a West Alpine group reached this island. The cache included two fine socketed celts, a fragment of what may have been a winged adze, fragments of two types of spearhead and pieces of sword blades and bits of mountings with rivets. Other finds were just lumps of bronze. Part of the hoard is at County Hall, Chelmsford, the rest at the Priory Museum.

These Bronze Age people who knew the area a thousand years before Christ were agriculturalists and could spin, weave and make pottery. They wore beads and personal ornaments of metal and stone and cremated their dead, although no funerary urns have yet been found in Basildon.

Cordierite-biotite-hornfels implement   Central Museum, Southend on Sea

Part of the Vange hoard

Central Museum, Southend on Sea

In a field called Sandhills, near Vange Hall, pieces of Roman brick and tile have been found and it is thought that a tile works once stood on the site. Roman remains have been found at Thundersley and Canvey, so it is reasonable to suppose that there was a villa or small settlement at Vange, the site being on one of a chain of low hills above the swamps that are now marshland.

No material traces of Anglo-Saxon occupation have been found, but the names Basildon, Laindon, Nevendon, Pitsea and Vange are of Saxon origin. Three contain personal names or tribe names: Basildon is 'Beorhtel's Hill'; Pitsea 'the island of Pic'; Nevendon 'Hnefa's valley'. Vange means 'fen district', the termination 'ge' indicating an early origin.

Great Chalvedon Hall from Rectory Road in the 1920s

Great Chalvedon Hall, once a manor and farm of some 600 acres, standing a little way off Rectory Road, Pitsea, is a 16th century house with many old beams, an ancient fireplace and an authentic secret room. It is now an hotel.

The old English name 'Chalvedon' means 'calves' hill' and the history of the manor goes back 800 years. In 1168 Chalveduna is recorded as making a contribution towards the marriage of the daughter of Henry II.

Ailward, a chamberlain of Henry's, came into possession of Chalvedon in 1177 and he had a chapel there sometime between then and 1179, for which he was granted a licence by Abbot Walter and the Convent of Colchester, for the Rectory of Pitsea belonged to them. Of this nothing remains except the name of Chapel Field, to the east of the house.

Subsequently the Fitz Walter family were the lords of Chalvedon. The Priory of St Mary Spittle or St Mary without Bishopsgate held Chalvedon of Robert Fitz Walter, who died in 1328. Spitalfields takes its name from this hospital and Spital Yard and Spital Square now cover its site. In 1274 the prior of the 'New Hospital without Bishopsgate' held a fair and market at Chalvedon.

At the Dissolution Chalvedon was granted to Thomas, Lord Cromwell, by Henry VIII. Later it returned to the Crown to become part of the dowry of Princess Mary. In February, 1562, Queen Elizabeth gave the estate to Thomas, Duke of Norfolk.

John Purland lived at Chalvedon Hall in 1585. Elizabeth Purlevant, who died in 1588, and to whose memory there is a brass inscription in Pitsea Church, was probably John's wife. A later tenant was Reynold Diglett in 1618.

The land was farmed until the Great War and Rectory Road from the old Rectory (now the site of the new Parish Church) was a very lonely road, the only habitation besides Chalvedon Hall being a farmworker's cottage just before the entrance to the Hall was reached and there were no more buildings until Burnt Mills Farm at the end of the road.

On the Arterial Road, near the factory sites, stands a picturesque farmhouse, a survival of old Basildon and typical of many former farmhouses in the area. Great Wasketts Farm derives its name from the family of Elyas Waskett of Writtle, who lived here in 1274. Since 1872 the Gardiner family have farmed Great Wasketts and have given their name to the road that runs by it, Gardiner's Lane.

Originally built in the Tudor era the house then only had 5 rooms. There are big ceiling beams, brick floors and a large brewhouse, which appears to have been detached from the house and was probably the kitchen, as before 1600 kitchens were often built separately from the house because of the fire risk.

There is still a hook over the chimney in the brewhouse for hanging joints to roast and a brick over for baking bread, which has not been used for a century. There is also a large copper and an antique sink with a pump by it. Over part of the brewhouse is an apple loft.

In Regency times the farmer decided to bring the house up to date and built on to the Tudor front five lofty rooms with a verandah. Reflected in the big horse pond the house makes a charming picture.

In 1649 William Wakefield, a London merchant, sold to Thomas Sharpp of Basildon, Wasketts and three woods called Bacons and Barwicks, 'now defaced and unwooded'. Sharp's Lane, recorded in 1667, has become Gardiner's Lane.

In 1688 Wasketts supplied fuel to London as Anna Wilkinson of Crutched Friars, London, leased to Monjoy Harwood, of St Andrew's, Holborn, wood merchant, wood and underwoods belonging to Wasketts, excepting trees (only lops were leased) with certain liberties to hew trees. The lessee was allowed 'to make small cole [charcoal]' in convenient places.

In 1932 the Arterial Road disturbed the ancient peace of Wasketts by cutting across the meadow in front of the house.

Wasketts, farm, 1962

Dunton Wayletts

At Dunton, on the edge of the New Town, standing at a crossroads, is a 400 year old farmhouse with massive chimneys, known as Dunton Wayletts. Once the front of this quaint old house had an overhanging upper storey, but it still has a charming old staircase and some 17th century panelling.

In 1603 George Drywood held Dunton Wayletts from King's College, Cambridge. In *The History of Essex, by a Gentleman* 1769-72 it is stated that in Dunton Churchyard there was a monument to Richard Green, gentleman, which was erected in 1690 by Elizabeth, his wife. There are several weather-worn tombstones remaining, but Richard's can no longer be identified. The entry in the burial register reads, 'Richard Green of the Waylet dyed January 25, 1689, and was buried January 31. Affidavit brought the 7th of Ffeb 1689'. The affidavit was made that the body had been buried in woollen cloth, according to the Woollen Act of 1678.

The name Waylett means a place where roads meet and here in 1280 Gundreda atte Weylete lived. Opposite the farm is a green lane that was probably in those days a highway and Gundreda got her name from living at the crossroads. On 2 February, 1280, Gundreda, the widow of William, son of Richard the Smith, formerly of Leyndon [Laindon], demised to the Master of St Bartholomew's Hospital, John Walton, a piece of meadow at Dunton for four years and he gave her 4s. Her seal bears a plant with seven branches.

Geoffrey of Eyston, Master of St Bartholomew's from 1281 to 1285 was granted by Gundreda a messuage which she had of the gift of Simon of Dunton, which stood 'on the king's way which leads from Horndon towards Chelmsford'. The Master and bretheren gave Gundreda 19s down 'in gersummam' [An entry fine on taking a tenement over].

William atte Weylate was among the witnesses to this grant. Some names of witnesses to Dunton charters of the 13th century are very interesting, such as John of the Meadow, Stephen of the Wood, Thomas le Herde, Gerard the Barber and Stephen le Bolde.

The name of Westley Hall is the only reminder that this part of Langdon Hills was a separate parish 500 years ago. West Lee, or Westley, belonged to the Dean and Chapter of St Paul's and in 1297 a visitation of the chapter's peculiars (churches exempt from ordinary ecclesiastical authority) was undertaken by the Dean, Ralph de Baldock, and certain assessors. On 14 September they arrived at West Lee, their business being to record the condition of the church, its furniture and ornaments. It was a poor parish and they found the church in a sad state. The revenue was too small to support a resident incumbent amd the church was in a ruinous condition.

Cattle were feeding in the churchyard, as the fence was broken down; the wooden font leaked and there was no lock to the cover; the windows of the nave were unglazed; and there was no bell. At the entrance to the church there should have been a holy water stoup with a sprinkler, but at West Lee there was a lead bason.

The church, however, had three full sets of vestments. That used on Sundays was of buckram with apparels of green samite (silk woven with gold thread).

Later no one would accept the benefice of West Lee as the revenue was too small to support a priest. It was, therefore, very neglected and the patrons besought the Bishop that it might be amalgamated with Langdon (Hills) and formal sanction was given on 22 July, 1432.

Langdon's rector entered at once upon the rectory of West Lee and he had to say Mass once a year in Westley Church on the feast of its dedication, but it soon fell into complete decay. Its exact location is unknown, but near the supposed site stands the 200 year old Westley Hall, no doubt a successor to an older house. Its ancient barn is said to incorporate timbers from the church.

Westley Hall barn, 1938

Chambers Farm, Nevendon, February, 1958

Just outside the Basildon boundary, not far from the industrial sites, stands the picturesque cottage of Chamber's Nurseries. Chambers got its name from an owner, Richard le Camber, the comb maker, who lived in 1319.

The weather-boarded house with its cosy thatched roof is, however, only about 300 years old, although the timber in it may be older, as it shows signs of previous use.

The small farm came under the manor of North Benfleet. John Rooe was admitted to Cambers on the death of his father in 1609 and John Powley, rector of Nevendon, was admitted tenant of Cambers in 'Nevingdon' in 1755. On his death in 1787 two heriots or fines due to the lord of the manor were needed. Two horses were seized, but on 12 October, 1787, Mrs Powley appeared before Mr Judd and paid compensation for them and was admitted tenant: part of the rent was a number of capons.

Not far from Chamber's, but just inside the Wickford boundary in Cranfield Park Road, stands a most interesting farmhouse that gives an excellent idea of the way the Tudors built many a former Basildon home. Great Broomfields probably got its name from the family of Hubert de Bromfield, 1285.

The house was built in the 16th century with a wing added the next century. When the weatherboarding that had been added later was removed the original wattle and daub between the beams was revealed on the oldest part. The twigs used as lathes were laced together with what appeared to be coarse grass. The daub of earth, hair, etc., was applied by two men standing on either side of the wall and both applying it to meet on the wattle. Roman numerals, carpenters' marks, cut on the exterior beams can still be seen.

The kitchen has an inglenook fireplace now fitted with a modern stove. A large quantity of oats were found in the ceiling of the former dairy during renovations, the room above having two floors.

Foreriders, Nevendon, February, 1958

On the Wickford Road near the Cricketers at Nevendon is a funny old house with an overhanging storey, whose history goes back 600 years. Traces can still be seen of the moat that formerly surrounded the house and which was a defence against attacks of both man and beast. This ancient property is known as Fore Riders, a name probably associated with Richard Forridere, who lived in 1327, although the house dates only from the 16th century.

Fore Riders and the surrounding land belonged in the 16th century to a monastic hospital or chantry chapel at Melton or Milton, near Gravesend. In 1524 Henry VIII granted it to Sir Henry Wyatt: it was then described as 'one messuage and 30 acres of arable land called Foreriders. Sheepcote with a garden. Sheephouse Field 6 acres. 30 acres, Upper Gayne Hill, Lower Gayne Hill. Suthfield or Drivers 26 acres, Bousfield and Alwynstond 42 acres, land called Paynters 8 acres'.

The field bordering the moat was called Moatfield. Alwynstond was probably corrupted into the field names of Great and Little Candlestick Hill. Other interesting field names in Nevendon were Row Leys (meaning rough pasture) and Burnt Mill Hill (recalling a medieval fire).

Langdon Hills had the attractive field names of Damson Mead, Reedy Pond Hill, Musket Hill, Broken Batch, Great and Little Oxcroft, Flax Field and Rye Field. Kiln Field refers to the brick workings that were there in the early 19th century.

In 1957 a number of names of roads in Basildon were changed to eliminate duplication. Many of the old names and some of the new have interesting historical associations.

The Chase at Vange was changed to Hill Farm Chase: originally this was the way to the 400 year old timber farmhouse, now demolished, that was recorded as long ago as 1345 as Le ffangehul.

Victoria Road, Vange, changed to Curtis Road, was laid out by R L Curtis at the end of the last century. His son, A P Curtis, JP, lived for many years nearby at Empire House, Brickfield Road.

When Pound Lane, Laindon, south of the Arterial Road, was renamed Doves Farm Road a memory of the village pound for straying cattle vanished. Pound field was opposite Doves Farm, which was owned by Charles Dove in 1839.

Pound Lane, Bowers Gifford, is also associated with a pound. An old Bowers Gifford resident used to say that a man riding a white horse haunted Pound Lane at midnight. She was terribly frightened when on one occasion she had to pass through the lane at that time, but she did not see the phantom rider. A pound is mentioned at Vange in 1598, but its location is unknown.

About 1600 Dry Street, Langdon Hills, is mentioned in a manorial rental. Simon Dale, in the right of his wife, Francis, held a half acre of land called Wythers or Wythards at 'Drystreet in Layndon' at a rent of 4d. The name 'street' may well indicate the the road is of Roman origin.

Pound Lane in the 1930s

Moat House and the farmer's family early this century. Name unknown

In Church Road, Basildon, near Holy Cross Recreation Ground, is an ancient moat and fishpond, a relic of early days. Until the 1950s the moat encircled Moat Farm, an early 19th century building succeeding a much earlier house.

This farm was also known as Botelers Manor, sometimes shown on ancient maps. Botelers was named after John Botill or Botiller of Walden who held it in 1362. Boteler is sometimes spelt butler and relates to that domestic office. John appears to have married Eleanor, the widow of a former occupier of the manor, Robert Travers, who died at Basildon in 1348/9. He left money to Holy Cross Church for masses to be said for the souls of members of his family.

In a grant of life interest at a rent of 27s.0d. for a Fobbing marsh called Southope in 1384 a dovecot or pigeon house in John Boteler's homestead at Basildon is mentioned. This was a valuable property that helped to fill the larder with pigeon pie and other savoury dishes.

In 1520 Elizabeth Torell, a widow, leased to Richard Batell, Elizabeth Rogerrys, widow, and Edmund Rudley the manor of Basildon, alias Botelers and a messuage called Unywantes (Oliphants, which stood near the old Rectory in Rectory Road) and the 'maner place called Butlerres'. Elizabeth Torell had to be responsible for repairs unless the tenants caused the property to be 'hurtyd broky or ympeyryd' and she had to provide 'fyrebote, plowbote, harow-bote and cartbote', which meant that she had to supply on demand wood for fuel, and repairs to ploughs, harrows and carts.

Hovefields, 1958

At the north end of Pitsea parish stands the former farm house known as Hovefields. The road approaching it (Hovefields Avenue) was once a long, lonely lane, probably 'the certain lane called Hallfellslane' mentioned in 1655, beside which was the croft of 3 acres called Reyners, held by Thomas Rayment for a yearly rent of sixpence.

The earliest mention of Hovefields was in 1421, since when it has been called Holfield, Holefelde, Howel's, Howfield, Holfield and, on the 1777 Chapman & André map, Hobbles. Sometimes it was pronounced 'Hovells' by the villagers. It means 'fold in the hollow'.

The land formerly belonging to Hovefields was in Nevendon as well as Pitsea: it was sold by William Fitz Lewis in 1522 to William Berdford. In 1661 Robert Bernard of Huntingdon sold it to Nicholas Pedley of Lincoln's Inn.

The front is about 200 years old, but the rear probably dates from a century earlier, with exposed ceiling beams. Eighty years ago all the farm buildings were destroyed by fire, now only the farm cottages and pond remain.

Another farm burnt down was Brick House Farm. The old red brick house, demolished in the 1930s, stood in High Road on the left hand corner of New Park Avenue, near Tescos. It had a kitchen wing of tarred timber with wooden window shutters. In 1834 it was known as Bricked House Farm and its 86 acres were leased to James Sparkes for 7 years at £90 a year. It was mentioned as part of the marriage settlement of Mary Ann, the betrothed of Joslin Bulwer of Brentwood in 1853.

The 1845 Tithe Map shows what appears to have been part of a moat near the house. This was the first farm sold for building development in Pitsea.

When the moat at Pitsea Hall was being cleared a Roundhead helmet was found in the mud in a good state of preservation, even the leather straps being intact. A number of bones were also dredged up, but it is not known if they were animal or human.

Pitsea Hall can be traced back to Domesday, when it was owned by the King, who gave it to the Norman lord Eudo Dapifer, who, in his turn, gave it to the Abbey of St John, Colchester, which he had founded.

In the Ministers' Accounts of 1421-2 there is record of building a dam at Pitsea Hall and of scouring the ditch between dry land and marsh towards Estle and cleaning the water pipe at the eastern end of the pond, near the stable. The livestock was 6 stotts (young bullocks), 10 rams, 155 ewes, 75 gimmers (ewes between 1st and 2nd shearing) and 22 lambs. Ploughs, ploughshares, carts and saddles, a waggon, riddle, dung fork and winnowing fan are listed.

In 1534 the Abbot of St John's leased Pitsea Hall to Edward Breton and Robert Pake. After the Dissolution of the Monasteries it became the property of Thomas, Lord Cromwell. On his attainder it reverted to the Crown and appointed for the maintenance of Princess Mary. Queen Elizabeth granted it to Thomas Howard, Duke of Norfolk, and, in 1581, it was conveyed to Roger Townshend and Edward Cooke; from the Cooke family it passed to the Moyers.

Originally there were 1,720 acres belonging to the Manor, but now only a marsh remains with the house, which dates from about 1600. One wing is half-timbered with an overhanging storey. There are massive ceiling beams and the kitchen still has its stone floor, hooks for hams and an old baker's oven. In Elizabethan times there were two dove houses on the estate.

When the railway reached Pitsea in 1854 it destroyed all the farm buildings, as the line cut through the farmyard. £2,250 compensation was paid to the owners, Rev G Heathcote and the Hon P Dawney.

Five hundred years ago the important Abbey of Barking held Hawkesbury Manor in Fobbing, now within the boundaries of Basildon. Court Rolls of this manor during the troubled reign of Henry VI give pictures of tenants conducting manorial business, probably in the hall of the manor house.

At a Court held on 6 November, 1454, all the homage (tenants who presented incidents to the Court) on behalf of Hawkesbury elected John Peers to the office of Collector of the Rents of the Lady [Abbess] for the coming year and John was sworn to do this service. In 1458 John was in trouble because he had not repaired the 'ruinous house in his bond tenure called Fullers' and he was fined in mercy 4d - which meant that the abbess fined him only the stated amount and not more heavily. At the same Court William Heggeman was elected as rent collector within the lordship of Hawkesbury.

The following year John Peers was again presented for making waste in 'Fulleres' by allowing the house to become greatly ruinous to the heavy damage of the tenement and he was fined 3d.

At the Court held in 1455 there is mention of a ditch overflowing at Dry Street. The homage presented that the lady abbess had not scoured the ditch next to the highway at 'Dreystrete next Hawkyns elme in length 80 perches to the annoyance of the people of the lord king'. The farmer of the manor, on behalf of the abbess, was ordered to clean the ditch before the next Leet Court under pain of a heavy penalty.

In 1459 there was more trouble: Robert Sprever, the farmer on behalf of the abbess, was ordered to scour the 'ladys ditch at Drystrete in length of 40 perches' before the next Court under pain of 6s.8d. to be forfeited to the lady.

Hawkesbury Bush, Fobbing, April, 1961

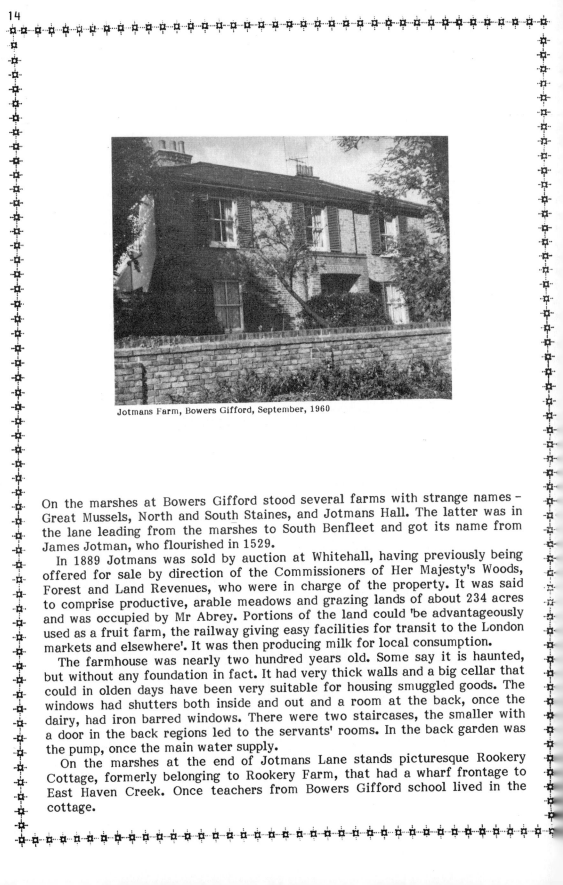

Jotmans Farm, Bowers Gifford, September, 1960

On the marshes at Bowers Gifford stood several farms with strange names – Great Mussels, North and South Staines, and Jotmans Hall. The latter was in the lane leading from the marshes to South Benfleet and got its name from James Jotman, who flourished in 1529.

In 1889 Jotmans was sold by auction at Whitehall, having previously being offered for sale by direction of the Commissioners of Her Majesty's Woods, Forest and Land Revenues, who were in charge of the property. It was said to comprise productive, arable meadows and grazing lands of about 234 acres and was occupied by Mr Abrey. Portions of the land could 'be advantageously used as a fruit farm, the railway giving easy facilities for transit to the London markets and elsewhere'. It was then producing milk for local consumption.

The farmhouse was nearly two hundred years old. Some say it is haunted, but without any foundation in fact. It had very thick walls and a big cellar that could in olden days have been very suitable for housing smuggled goods. The windows had shutters both inside and out and a room at the back, once the dairy, had iron barred windows. There were two staircases, the smaller with a door in the back regions led to the servants' rooms. In the back garden was the pump, once the main water supply.

On the marshes at the end of Jotmans Lane stands picturesque Rookery Cottage, formerly belonging to Rookery Farm, that had a wharf frontage to East Haven Creek. Once teachers from Bowers Gifford school lived in the cottage.

With the exception of the brass to Sir John Gifford at Bowers Gifford there are no memorials to members of noble families in any of the Basildon churches, for the great who owned the land did not live in the area and there were no large mansions, although it is rather surprising to find in an 1890 directory that Vange Hall is on the list of the principal seats of Essex, being then owned and occupied by Robert L Curtis.

At Fobbing there is an entry in the church register of the burial there of Dame Margaret Sackville, the last prioress of the Benedictine Nunnery of Eastbourne, 'ye iv day of Dec. 1540', but there is no memorial.

In Vange church there is an interesting monument to Mary, wife of a former rector, George Maule, who died in 1659. The inscription concludes: 'O, let thy cinders warme that bed of dust for mee, Thy mournful husband till I come to lie by thee'.

Tombstones in the village churchyards do not date back farther than the 18th century, with the exception of Holy Cross, Basildon, where there is a tiny headstone near the southeast corner of the chancel to Mary Betts, who died in 1662.

In the Hearth Tax Return for 1662 John Beates [sic] of Basildon had three hearths

North Benfleet has a stone just outside the church porch to a Waterloo warrior, John Cole, 'who at the celebrated command 'Up, Guards, and at 'em' was wounded by a musket ball, but heroically persevered till the victory'. He died in 1836, bequeathing his medal to the curate who erected the memorial.

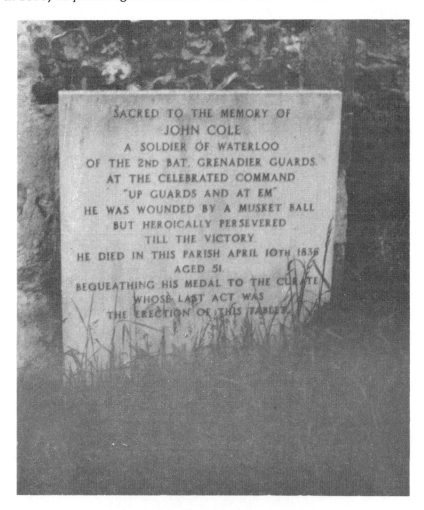

At Nevendon there is a tombstone with a gruesome inscription that was popular in the 18th century. The stone is to the memory of John Peck, who died in 1755, aged 41, and the just decipherable stone reads, 'Remember me as you pass by. As you are now, so once was I. As I am now, so must you be. Prepare yourself to follow me'.

Pitsea churchyard has a stone to a lady who is described as 'a weak and sinful worm the vilest of her race'.

There used to be 50 or more barns in the Basildon area, but fewer than 20 remain. In times past, when all the corn was home grown, Basildon people knew a good harvest was vital and every farm had a barn, a most important building in the medieval period, for a safe, weatherproof storage building was essential.

Most of the Basildon barns were timber-framed, faced with tarred weather-board and the roofs were often thatched. A pair of thatching shears from Tiffaynes Farm, North Benfleet, have been given to Canvey Island Museum.

Corn was often mentioned in wills. William Homfrey of Pitsea in 1559 left all his corn on the north side of the barn to be sold and the money 'endefferently' divided among his children.

Richard Spencer of Vange in his 1690 will left to his son, Richard, four bushels of wheat and one quarter of oats, which was owing to him by his son-in-law, Abraham Bennington, and his great brass kettle, in which he usually brewed, and his mashing tub (for mashing and malt brewing) and the two least of his drinking vessels.

William Sandell of Nevendon in 1542 left his wife all the wheat growing at 'Grynsbes' and 'all ye hottes [oats] yt shalbe sone upon my ground here', also ten quarters of wheat 'to kepe hyr huse wt'.

In Rectory Road at the Burntmills end is the 17th century barn originally belonging to Burntmills Farm, now a motor repair shop. The ancient beams, where housemartins still nest, looked down on the 'barnman', mentioned in the farm accounts of Thomas Sparkes, preserved at the Record Office. The barn-man threshed nine quarters, four bushels, of oats for 16s.7½d in 1811. He was also paid 7s.6d. for three days' work. For hoeing three 'ackers' of beans he had £1.4s.0d. 'Gun and his three mates for carting of straw out of the barn and setting up sheves' were paid the munificent sum of 2s. [10p]. In 1811 Sparkes paid 1s.6d. 'for a lock for the barn door at Burnt Mills Barn'.

Vagrants travelling from village to village often rested in barns: children were born there: and weary travellers died therein. In 1701 William Hill, Rector of Pitsea, wrote in the church register that 'John the son of John Robson, a traveller, was born in my neighbour Joselyne's barn April ye 9th, 1701 and was baptised upon ye 12th day of the same month'.

At Vange in December, 1624, 'a poor woman died in the Parsonage barn' and at Nevendon in 1765 a man was murdered in a barn at Little Bromfords.

When Christopher Powley became Nevendon's Rector in 1712 he found there was no barn, so he built one (now used as a church hall) to keep his tithes safe.

Barn, Burnt Mills Farm, Rectory Road, Pitsea, 1958

In 1588 John Sandell, evidently a man of substance living at Shonks Farm, Vange, left to his son, Thomas, 'all the glass in the windows round about the house.' In late Elizabethan times glass was still valuable and was probably in removeable frames fitted to the windows. Thomas was also left 'the joyned bedstead in the parlour as it standeth with all things thereto belonging' and a ship's chest, a table with a frame, a cupboard fastened to the wainscot, the wainscot or wooden panelling, with the settles in the parlour and the hall.

John's son, Richard, was left land called Almond Downe Newmans with the house and powlters [?poultry yard] and 'my Bargayne which I have at fange called Shonckes as I now hold and enjoy and all the corn, cattle, hay and other things belonging to ye said farme which are in my use occupyinge and possession'. In addition, Richard had £5 towards 'ye payment of this half year's rent at Michaelmas next' and a brown colt 'that was bought of James Fuller and the brown mare colt that came of my dun ambling mare'.

Shonks Farm ceased to be farmed at the turn of the century and now houses cover the site in High Road, east of the Barge Inn, nearly opposite Rickling. The ancient farm buildings in Whytewater Avenue used to include a fine barn.

Shonks is said to have derived its name from the family of John Shonke.

Former Shonks Farmhouse, 1959

Fanton Hall, North Benfleet, 1930

Before church registers were ordered to be kept in printed books of prescribed forms in 1813 many interesting facts were often added to entries.

There is a record of a murder at Fanton Hall, North Benfleet –

> Andrew Welsh (by Coroner's Inquisition returned murthered by Richard Kaminhaugh which was also sworn before me) buried August the 5th 1734. Kaminhaugh escaped after ye fact committed at Fanton Hall thence immediately.

The history of Fanton Hall manor goes back to before the Conquest when part of it was held by Alestan Stric. In 1086 it belonged to Westminster and Barking Abbeys. Alestan's part was claimed for the King's use on the grounds that it came to Westminster Abbey by a forged writ, the Abbey being notorious for this kind of document.

In 1679-80 Lady Ann Fanshawe left in her will to her 'deare son Sir Richard Fanshawe' her lease of the manor of 'Faunton Hall', which she held of the Bishop of London. Lady Ann, a much-travelled and accomplished woman, never lived in Essex. Her husband, also Sir Richard, was an eminent diplomatist and poet. A Royalist, he was taken prisoner at the Battle of Worcester, but in the reign of Charles II he was Ambassador to Spain. By 1768 Fanton Hall belonged to John Russell.

The Bishop of London leased the Hall to the nobility who, in turn, let it to farmers who lived on the land, such as Robert Drywood in 1565 and Nathaniel Gilman in 1645. Nathaniel did not scour 100 rods of ditch lying between Fanton Hall and Great Wheatleys Farm in Rayleigh 'to the drowning and overflowing' of a great quantity of grounds of Wheatleys Farm occupied by John Offin.

Fantons residents in the 16th century were responsible for the repair of the churchyard fence 'from the great elme on the East to the Churchyard Gate at the South-East corner, three rods, ten feet and on the South side six rods, two foote'.

The name Fanton is Old English meaning the farm by the marsh. The 300 year old farmhouse was demolished over 50 years ago.

Some of the oldest businesses in Basildon were the village smithies. At Vange Bells the smithy is mentioned in title deeds of 1690 as 'a smith's shop or fforge lately in tenure of Thomas Iore and now of the churchwardens and overseers of the parish of Vange'. In 1786 Philip West, the Vange blacksmith, also held the Five Bells at a yearly rent of £14.8s.0d.

Robert Crooks was the blacksmith at Pitsea in 1890, while mention is made of a blacksmith named Robert Walsbecke at Pitsea in 1651. Robert probably had a forge occupying the site later known as The Gables. Pitsea Church registers record that on Easter Day, 29 March, 1741, William Middleton, 'black Smith of Pitsey', was buried and, on 19 May, 1742, William Middleton, 'son of the Blacksmith of Pitsey', was interred.

At Bowers Gifford A A Markham's busy forge is said to date from 1600. Its smoke-blackened timbers have seen many smiths, including Stephen Ransom in 1848 and George Thomas Upson in 1890.

At the corner of Dunton Road and High Road, Laindon was another smithy, said to be over 200 years old and in the same family for 60 years. Thomas Newman came from Danbury to take over the forge formerly belonging to the old Fortune of War Inn standing nearby. In 1848 Christopher Blanks was the blacksmith and shopkeeper at Laindon.

In 1848 Dunton had a blacksmith, Jerimiah Collins, who also kept a shop. At the same time the Langdon Hills smith was James Cockerell. During the last century there was a forge in Bull Road, Basildon.

High Road, Pitsea, 1960. The old blacksmith's is on the left

Gipsies have always favoured the Basildon area and are sometimes seen encamped near the New Town. The Bowers Gifford parish registers tell the sad tale of Ludovic and Mary, twin children of 'a travelling woman (commonly called a Gypsye)' who were baptised on 21 September, 1690, and a week later were buried in one coffin.

In 1886 a large number of gipsies were permanently located on Laindon Common and it was considered unsafe to go in Frith Wood. A London newspaper of 1901 gave a graphic picture of gipsies at Laindon who had been threatened with eviction by the Billericay Rural Council.

'Laindon is the last word in the dreary history of distressed agriculture in Essex,' it was stated. 'Parcelled out into fields and meadows by unkempt hedgerows are thousands of acres whose plentiful crop of thistles tells its own melancholy tale.'

The gipsies had encamped 'on one of these building plots above the little village where the few houses seem to have dropped down casually on the landscape'. Most of them 'belonged to the great Bibby family which supply cocoanut shies and roundabouts to the country fairs from Yeovil to Maldon'.

The older women wore brilliant home-knitted vests and smoked short clay pipes or chewed tobacco. They would tell your fortune if you were not a policeman in disguise and were keen of wit. Soup simmered in a huge open pot over an open fire and tasted like rabbit broth. A lurcher 'seemed good enough to account for a hare'.

One of the Bibby family showed the inside of his caravan, which had a gleaming brass stove and two beds arranged like ships' bunks. He and 'the old girl' and three 'kids' slept there as comfortable as anybody.

He said they did nothing to the villagers to frighten them, except that some of them had broken the lid of a well to get water. Water was the difficulty, but it was the same everywhere, hardly any wells and no water supply.

Later, many gipsies camped permanently on building land at Vange.

Gipsies at Dunton, 1956

An old farm account book, originally belonging to the Pocklington family of Vange Hall that was in use from 1773 to 1852, gives interesting facts and figures on life in Vange two hundred years ago. As well as farm accounts it has records of household expenses, parish accounts, receipts for payments, cures for animal ailments and a copy of an old ballad. The spelling is often phonetic and the calculations are sometimes incorrect.

Thomas Pocklington, who farmed in a fairly large way, moved to Vange from Kinoulton in Nottinghamshire in 1827 and a page is headed: 'Paid at Vange. Going to see it three Tims £10.0s.0d. October 9th/10th. Expencis coming to it £12.0s.' Thomas also spent £1.10s.0d at Vange Bells.

Further items from the same page are 'For beer from Stanford-le-Hope, £1; a leg of Mutton, 6s; Moles 1s; Beef £1.2s.3d; Tea, Sugar £1.17s; Expences to London 13s.8d; Candles, 2s.8d; Plough Driver, 14 days at 6d, 7s; Coach higher [hire] to Leicester, £2.2s.'

In 1827 butter was 1s.4d a pound and cheese 6d. Other interesting entries are

1827	Nov 22 – Plow driver, 17 days	8.6d
	Dec 7 – Southend sale	42.0.0d
1828	Jan 8 – Crown Brewery, Billericay	8.0.0d
	March 26 – Letter	1.4d
1849	June 4 – Paid at Stanford-le-Hope at the King Hed	10.0d
1851	March 22 – Poor Rate Vange	3.12.0d
	April 19 – Going to Romford	1.0d
	April 19 – Tolbar	6d
	April 19 – 10 wagen Lodes of gravel from Tilborough	1.0.0d
	July 26 – To half year's Propperty Tax Due 25th March, 1851	3.13.7½d
	Oct 9 – Blaxsmith Pitsey Wagen	2.12.11d

There is also a note that in 1829 Thomas Pocklington agreed with the Overseers of Vange to take Joseph Marsh at 2s.6d a week and clothe him. Thomas was, at different times, a churchwarden, Overseer and Surveyor of the Highways.

1827	Patt at Tange			
	Going to see it three Tims	10	10	
Ocr 9-10	Expencis ßorming to it	12	10	
	Mr Cole as Prais	307		
	Meet Beef 1.1.4 Mutto 4.4	1	9	9
	at Tange Bells	1	10	
	Billireckey Markets	1	8	
14	Expen to London		6	2
	Mr Cole Sow Souls Bricks	10	17	
16	Markets 4/3 Expen 4/½		8	4½
	Aroe Bonsh		10	
17	Laver Stones 14 Role Harrers Cart	14	8	6
	Carte Mash Tubs Plow 10.6			
	Tollows Freakly 3 Beesoms 5 Satt 5 Cant 4		13	3
	Lanton			
19	Ale Gurl servant 2.6 Months 1		5	6
20	Leg of Mutton		6	
	Clatom 9 days Work at 2		18	
	Moles		1	
21	Beef 2.3 Tea Sugar 7.17 Expenses to London 13	3	12	3
	Cart Higher to Leicester	2	2	0
	Dogs Candles 2/8 Moles 2/-		5	8
27	Clatom 6 days work 2/-		12	0
	David		15	0
	Plough Driver 14 days at 6		7	0
Nov 3	Clayton 4 week		12	0
	at a Sale			
	Markets 2/4 Hat 7/0 Tobben 1/2		9	5½

Laindon Ponds, 1963

In times past some six farmsteads and cottages were the only buildings to be seen in Wash Road, Laindon, on the northern edge of Basildon, a stone's throw from the Arterial Road and the New Town.

The most important was Laindon Ponds, shown on Chapman and André's 1777 map. The timber-frame house still has a large part of its wide, deep moat. The front has been altered in later years, but still has 18th century sash windows and inside are many exposed ceiling beams, some ships' timbers, old latched doors and sloping bedroom floors. Not so long ago there was another wing to the south. In the garden is the old well and there is a romantic, but highly improbable, tradition of an underground passage running to Laindon Church.

Laindon Ponds is no longer farmed and all the farm buildings have gone; the 1839 tithe map shows 19 fields with a total of 149 acres: some of the more interesting names being Pagel Mead (pagel is the old Essex name for 'cowslip'), Slip (a long narrow field) and the quaint Little Jack in the Wood (a name going back to 1570).

In 1839 Laindon Ponds was owned by Henry Soames and farmed by Charles Buckenham. By 1890 Eldred Buckenham farmed it and many descendants still live in Laindon.

Near the Wash is another farmhouse, Daniels, about the same age as Laindon Ponds. Daniels has a mansard roof and inside are old beams and quaint iron fireplaces in the bedrooms. Daniels is mentioned in a 1484 will as Danyell land.

As late as 1923 Wash Road had two other ancient farmhouses – Puckles Farm of the 17th century (on its site a house called 'The Lodge' now stands) and Petcheys Farm, of the same date, which stood on the site of a bungalow of the same name east of the Prince of Wales.

At the corner where Honeypot Lane meets Pipps Hill Road stood the buildings of Parsonage Farm, formerly the Rectory, burnt down in the late 1860s. Here, in the reign of George III, lived John and Mary Bruce who, in 15 years, had eight children, four of them dying in infancy.

On 23 August, 1778, 'Mary, daughter of John and Mary Bruce of Laindon Parsonage' was baptised. On 3 May, 1780, William, son of John and Mary, described in the church registers as 'farmers', was also baptised. William lived nearly three months, being buried on 30 July, 1780. In May, 1782, they had another child, Ann, and on 3 August, 1783, John was born. He lived only two months and was buried on 14 October. Three years later another John was baptised, but he lived only five weeks. On 20 May, 1788 yet another baby arrived to be called Charles (he survived).

Then, on 30 January, 1791, they decided to name the latest arrival John. This third John lived for 7 months and must have given his parents hope of at last having a John in the family, but by a strange coincidence he was buried on the same day and month as the second John, 4 September.

The old superstition that to name a child after one that had recently died was unlucky, because the dead child would come and call the living away, certainly appeared to come true in this family.

One more child was born to John and Mary; Rebecca in May, 1793. On 22 October, 1797, the father, John Bruce, was buried.

There is another record of a baby born at the Parsonage: unfortunate Susanna, the illegitimate child of Sarah Boddington (probably a servant) was baptised in June, 1786.

In 1800 there occurred the tragedy of Elizabeth, infant daughter of Edward and Mary Bruce, who was burnt at Laindon Parsonage, according to John Bell, the curate who buried her on 4 December.

Parsonage Farm buildings, Pipps Hill, 1960

In the late 18th century Basildon farmers usually had families of six or more children. Basildon church registers record the baptisms of members of the Jerry family, who lived at the moated manor house of Basildon Hall. The house has gone and the moat, now drained, is surrounded by East Thorpe, Clickett Hill and Rayside. Until 60 years ago it was a lonely place in open fields away from Church Road.

On 8 April, 1777, Elizabeth, daughter of Erasmus and Elizabeth Jerry, was baptised. On 14 July, 1778, William, son of William and Anne Jerry, was baptised: two days later he was buried.

There is a long entry in one of the church registers about this family –

> January 22, 1772, William of William and Ann Jerry, of Basildon born and baptised there. August 30, 1779, Erasmus Jerry was born at Hirton in Suffolk and privately baptised there. Ann Jerry born at Basildon April 23, 1781, and privately baptised there May 6, 1781. W.P. curate. John Jerry born October 2, 1784, at Fobbing and privately baptised there the same year: Mary Jerry born December 21, 1787, at Fobbing and privately baptised there, these four were fully christened January 22, 1792, at Basildon chapel and Sarah, daughter of the above William and Ann born November 2, 1791, was fully baptised the same time by me, William Potter, curate.

Basildon Hall at the same time sheltered other families. John Carter, an Irish labourer, died there in October, 1779. On 11 March, 1787, Thomas, son of Thomas and Rebecca Claxon, 'lodgers at Basildon Hall', was baptised. Mary, daughter of William and Mary Hearne of Basildon Hall, was baptised 4 June, 1786. The Hearnes probably farmed there, while the Jerrys were at Fobbing or in Suffolk.

There is a story that when the old Basildon Hall (not the most recent building) was derelict before it was destroyed by fire, a horse got inside and walked up the stairs, starting a rumour that the house was haunted.

Basildon Hall
moat, 1939

The name of Fairhouse School in Church Road, Basildon, is a reminder of a once well-known farm that stood on the site. Somewhere near here was held Basildon Fair on 14 September. In 1871 Palin in *Stifford and its Neighbourhood* stated that there was a meadow called the Fair Field in which 'until comparitively recent times cattle used to be bought and sold'.

Fairhouse Farm at one time stood further up the road towards the church, but was rebuilt where the school now stands in the 19th century. The farm house was demolished just before World War II. The servants' bedroom was entirely cut off from the rest of the upper storey, having a separate staircase and no other means of access.

In the 18th century the Mead family farmed Fairhouse and the baptisms of six Mead children are recorded in the Basildon Church registers. On 1 February, 1784, James, son of James and Elizabeth Mead 'at the Fairhouse', was baptised and on 7 January, 1787, Sarah; 10 May, 1789, Mary; 6 November, 1791, George; 20 April, 1794, John; and 12 November 1797, Susannah.

James and Elizabeth suffered a tragic fate. The church registers record that, as they were riding home from Romford Market in 1808, their horse was frightened at the fifteenth milestone by the shouting of the postillions on a gentleman's coach and got out of control. The light cart in which they were travelling overturned and the coach passed over them both, killing James immediately, Elizabeth lingering for a few hours.

There are several more entries in the registers mentioning Fairhouse. On 29 December, 1779, John Lowen from Fairhouse, aged 64, was buried. His wife, Elizabeth, died the following March. John was a day labourer and apparently, as was then the practice, lived in the farmhouse buildings.

On 27 October, 1780, 'a lodger from the Fairhouse by name Saml Howard, aged 27' was buried. 'John... a lodger from the Fair House, pauper,' was buried on 26 November 1792.

Fairhouse Farm, 1930s

A smugglers' path runs from Hadleigh Castle, through Vange and Pitsea, to Fobbing. It was used by a meinie known as the Essex Gang, of whom Dick Turpin, the highwayman, was a member. They made their headquarters in Hadleigh Castle and the curious were frightened away from the ruins by ghostly lights of coloured fire, giving the area a reputation for being haunted.

The path avoided the villages and kept to the lonely marshes. The railway now runs by its side to Pitsea, where the path crosses Station Lane and the railway and goes over Pitsea and Vange Marshes, past Vange Wharf and the present swimming pool and Gouldings Farm, to Fobbing, a well-known smugglers' trading post.

Nevendon Hall has secret passages said to have been used by the smugglers. There was a local tradition that when the place was built in 1789 it was boarded up so that passers-by could not see what was going on. The passages go up into the roof or down into the cellar by means of ladders. P Piggot, now living at High Wycombe, remembers as a boy going up them many years ago. One passage between the walls to the loft was entered by a sliding panel from one of the front rooms; another led up between the walls from one of the bed-rooms on to the roof, also through a sliding panel.

At Bowers Gifford the creek at Earls Hall, a lonely place where it was said 'vessels of good burthen' could come up, may have been used for contraband. Bowers Gifford Hall, built by the Spitty family in 1828, has a concealed stair-way. From the windowless attic the stairs go down between the wall and the back stairs. Once they led to the big cellar. Doubtless the entrances from both cellar and attic were well hidden. Lost in dust and cobwebs the existence of these stairs was unsuspected until recently.

When some panelling upstairs in this same house was removed, long strips cut from an 18th century account book were found pasted beneath layers of wallpaper. On these are records of bottles of wine and gallons of spirits. Sadly only one personal name can be deciphered and the information is very fragmentary. It is said that on several pieces that have since disappeared local rectors were named and a ship, the *Jane*.

These accounts may refer to contraband goods. Mr Sparkes 'Northben[fleet]' had [r]um and one gallon French brandy. In North Benfleet is the tombstone of Thomas Spakes who died in 1780. A descendant, another Thomas, held Bradfields Farm in 1834.

From the account slips it can be learnt that from 1768 to 1772 red and white port, Jamaica rum, Dutch gin, French brandy and rum shrub were all supplied. Some went as far into Essex as Hatfield Broad Oak, where £3.10s.0d worth of spirits was sold. The name of London can also be discerned. Brandy cost 8s. and 12s. a gallon and rum 9s. and 10s.6d a gallon.

Nevendon Hall, 1955
Bowers Gifford Hall, 1960

There are still a few old domestic buildings left in and around the New Town, although the old Basildon parish has nothing left but two homestead moats and the century-old Rectory. One of the oldest houses was Laindon Hall, now destroyed by fire and vandals, near St Nicholas Church, dating from the time of the Wars of the Roses.

The 16th century Chalvedon Hall in Rectory Road, Pitsea, was once a manor house surrounded by about 600 acres of good corn-growing land. In the first half of the 19th century eight teams of horses were kept at this farm.

Most of the old houses and cottages in the area contain huge beams and other period features. At Laindon Hall there was a fine Elizabethan oak staircase. The larger farms had gloomy back stairs for the servants.

At Vange Hall a little stairway led from the passage near the kitchen to one small servant's room only and at Fairhouse Farm there was a similar arrangement with a hatch communicating with the next bedroom, but no door.

Near the 200 year old Five Bells Inn at Vange are two old farm labourers' cottages that have been modernised. These and other cottages at Nevendon, Pitsea and Bowers Gifford, have small lean-to bedrooms at the rear, the ceiling sloping down sharply to the floor. The old Essex people refer to these rooms where the children, the single lodger or the husband if his wife was ill, slept, as 'gander hutches'.

The old cottages and schoolroom by Vange Rectory gates are about a century old, although they appear to be older. Rev. E Sendall received a grant of the land from Sir Charles Smith, lord of the manor and patron, on which to build a school and two cottages in 1858.

Typical thatched cottage with lean-to at Pitsea. It stood on the south side of the London Road, near the Prohibition, 1930

Paynters Hill, Vange, June, 1951. Note the fine elm trees

When the ancient elms surrounding Pitsea Church were cut down in 1959 it was a reminder that between 1815 and 1817 the Archdeacon of Essex inspected Pitsea Churchyard and noted 14 pollarded elms there. He also inspected Vange churchyard, counting 11 elms, 11 pollarded elms and one ash.

Trees planted in the Town Centre go towards replacing the many that have had to give way to the growth of the district. Once most Basildon roads were tree-lined. There was an avenue of elms in Timberlog Lane. High Road, Pitsea, to the east of Vange Working Men's Club was shaded with graceful wych elms.

There was a hundred year old pear tree in front of the old house opposite Howard Park, but this is now covered by the new road. Many of the old farm gardens contain ancient fruit trees.

There were, some years ago, in the garden of Goldings Farm, Vange, on the edge of the marshes, two yew trees that may have been there when a Dutchman lived there in the 17th century.

There is a legend that Paynters Hill, Vange, gets its name from a man of that name who hanged himself on an ash tree that still stood at the end of the last century. If this was so, Paynter must have committed suicide 300 years ago, as the name goes back at least to 1667.

Trees were used to mark the old parish boundaries. At Hawkesbury Bush, off Bell Hill Road, in 1768 it was said, 'some trees here have been a seamark.'

Dry Street Farmhouse is over two hundred years old, maybe more. The kitchen has hooks where hams used to hang and the remains of an old bread oven. This charming old house has a history for it was a cradle of Methodism.

A hundred and eighty years ago Methodists had little chance to worship in Essex, but in 1813 Henry Smith came from London to South Ockendon and built a chapel, to which came Methodists from the surrounding villages, including Dry Street hamlet. Families took their food for the day and travelled together on the homeward journey as far as possible.

Then a Yorkshire farmer named Wrigglesworth came to Dry Street Farm; he was a staunch Methodist who had been turned out of his Yorkshire holding because he held services in his home. At Dry Street he welcomed Methodist preachers to his home and services were held in the room to the left of the front door of the house as you enter. The preacher at the first service on 4 November, 1834, was John P Haswell, superintendent of Southwark circuit and many famous men have subsequently preached in this room. Immediately over the preaching room was the 'Prophet's Chamber' consigned to the use of the visiting preachers who, before the coming of the railway to Stanford-le-Hope, had a difficult journey to Dry Street.

Ministers came from Dartford and Gravesend alternately once a month, getting across the Thames by rowing boat. The visiting Minister crossed from Gravesend on Wednesday afternoon, walked to East Tilbury to preach and stay overnight. The next day, after visiting and dining, he walked to Stanford-le-Hope and on Friday reached Dry Street. After spending the night at the farm he would be driven by Mr Wrigglesworth to Stanford, then he had a 6 mile walk to Tilbury Ferry, reaching Gravesend about midday.

Now a Methodist Church stands near the old farmhouse.

Drystreet Farm, 1963

Pitsea parish accounts contain an item, 8d, paid for the Queen's Proclamation on 5 July, 1837. In the early days of Victoria's reign farm labourers attended church wearing smocks, holidays were unknown and entertainments few. A travelling 'wild beast' show at Stanford-le-Hope was an event. Some Vange farmers played cricket and a field on Vange Hall was known as Cricket Field.

The photograph shows Victor Wiles from Goldings Farm in about 1907 with his two horses and tumbril. The small child in the tumbril is holding the reins.

Before the London, Tilbury & Southend Railway came through Pitsea the nearest railway was at Brentwood. A Vange labourer walked to Brentwood and back to see a train for they were a novelty for natives of his area.

Vange Hall Cottages, now demolished, near All Saints' Church, were an example of late Victorian cottage architecture, being built for brickfield workers in 1883.

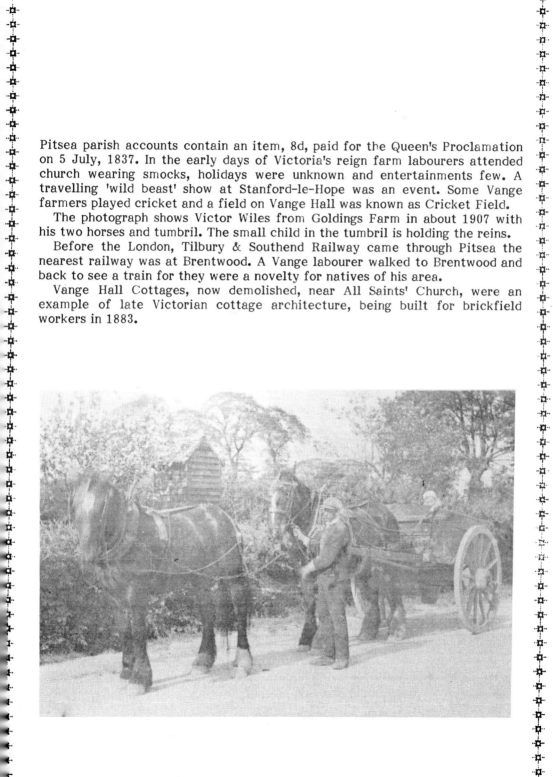

Hardly any adults in Vange could read or write in 1839. There was only a Sunday School, where 18 boys and 12 girls were taught in the church. A seraphine (a wind instrument having keyboard, windchest and bellows) accompanied the singing. Funds were difficult to procure, the Rector stated 'a narrow and grudging spirit prevailed in the parish'. Later a church school was built at the Rectory gates: the schoolroom with diamond paned windows still exists.

A tombstone in Nevendon churchyard tells that Elizabeth Kirkham, who died in 1788, was mistress of a school at Nevendon for 27 years. About 1850 a cowman's wife kept a school in a cottage in the lane to Basildon. Later a school was held in a thatched cottage that stood opposite the turning to Burnt Mills Road. The teacher, Mrs Atkins, could only make her mark in the register when she married, so she is unlikely to have taught writing! Then the Rev W M Kerr opened a school in the Tithe Barn and, in 1886, a National School was built.

In the 'Priest's House' at Laindon Church until 1881 Laindon and Basildon children were educated by Puckle's Charity: the last schoolmaster, James Hornsby, who had previously been a farm worker, is buried outside his old school. In 1877 a Board School was built in Laindon.

Until this century Pitsea children attended Bowers Gifford Church School, but in 1860 there was a Dame School at Bull Farm, Pitsea. The late Mrs Upson remembered attending it and sitting on the lower step of the stairs learning her lessons.

Bull farm house, 1948

Kingswood Farm, or Little Vange Hall, Bells Hill, Vange, April, 1961

Kingswood Hall in Bells Hill Road gives its name to a town neighbourhood, but formerly it was known as Little Vange Hall and, in the last century, as Bullocks Lodge. In the accounts of Bassom, plumber, glazier and house and ornamental painter, etc., of Billericay now at the Essex Record Office is a specification and estimate for painting at Little Vange Hall in April, 1840, for £17.2s.0d. The firm of Bassoms is still in business in a 16th century house in Billericay.

The name Brett, from Little Vange Hall, occurs in Vange church registers in 1839 and, in the 1851 Census Returns, the head of the house at Bullocks Lodge, was Thomas Kempster, aged 50, an agricultural labourer, who had been born at Langdon Hills: his wife, Teresa, who was 54, was born in Dorset, her birthplace being given as 'Swanetch'. The other people in the house on the night of 30 March, 1851, were Ann Harden, aged 55, a visitor, also born at Swanage; and John Roach, lodger, aged 52, whose birthplace was Vange.

Mr Belcham, who came to Bells Hill from Rayleigh in 1877, told his former employer it was 'a God-forsaken place'. By his efforts a meeting was held at Kingswood Hall when 60 people attended and Vange Mission came into being. In 1886 the Mission Church on Bell Hill was built; it was undenominational and with no ties with any other church. Mr Belcham was its first superintendent. Local people clubbed together and bought him a horse and trap, owing to the scattered and difficult nature of his 'parish'.

Station Lane, Pitsea, 1920s

In the last century, when the railway was built, there was a complete change of face for the ancient manor of Pitsea Hall. All the farm buildings were destroyed and the station was built on their site, almost under the farmhouse windows. The present house was built at the end of the 16th century, probably after the manor became the property of Roger Townshend and Edward Cook. In the next century it came into the possession of the Moyer family, one of whom, Sir Samuel, was a rich merchant who was Sheriff of the County in 1698.

In the 18th century the village pound for straying cattle was near the house, where Manor Courts were held in the hall, when transfer of property, trespass and similar business was conducted.

Station Lane was the original road to the Manor and a shop at the High Road end stands on the site of the gatekeeper's lodge.

Smuggling was said to be carried on at Pitsea Hall, the contraband goods being hidden in a pit in the yard with a huge kennel, complete with fierce dog, placed over it.

In the 1890s the hall pond was used for skating parties from Southend.

Last century farm workers from Pitsea Hall could have a pint at a little beerhouse called The Jerry, a timber cottage on the east corner of Northlands Drive. Pitsea is also said to have had a beerhouse called The Live and Let Live possibly the same place.

North Benfleet, just outside the boundaries of Basildon, is still a virtually un-changed country village. On the corner of Pound Lane and Burnt Mills Road stands ancient Pump Cottage which had a remarkable escape from demolition after being badly damaged by fire in 1961. It was formerly known as Clapper-gate Farm, probably from the swing gate standing nearby, but was later named from the nearby village pump. It is about 400 years old and once had a huge open fireplace. Within living memory farm buildings stood behind the cottage.

Horseshoe Cottage, 1961

Further along Pound Lane, at the corner of Harrow Road, stands Horseshoe Cottage, once the home of the village blacksmith. This pretty building is about three centuries old and originally two dwellings and incorporating the smithy. Each cottage had a living room, small bedroom and a 'backhouse' (Essex word for back quarters or scullery). A coin of the reign of Charles II has been found in the gardens.

In Harrow Road stood the old Harrow Inn and, at its side where the village hall is now, was the blacksmith's shop.

In School Lane stands the 1862 school, still in use. In 1890 48 children attended the school. Frederick Crick was the blacksmith (Crick's Corner at the junction of Pound Lane and Harrow Road is named after him), Frederick Dorman kept the Harrow and Henry Webb was the postmaster and kept the village store. Letters arrived from Bowers Gifford at 8.45 and were despatched daily at 4.20 The nearest money order office was a Wickford and the telegraph office was at Wickford Station.

About a hundred years ago the occupier of one of the two cottages that are now Horseshoe Cottage was fond of visiting the Harrow. One evening his wife threatened that if he returned home late she would lock him out. Undaunted, he took the door off its hinges and carried it along to the Harrow with him!

Well Green Cottages, 1963

To walk up Dry Street to Langdon Hills was like going back in time, the narrow, winding road not having altered much since the last century. A tiny, one-storey thatched cottage crouched behind a hedge and, further up, another ancient homes and the picturesque farmhouse and buildings of Blackman's or Hasted's Farm. The Post Office was formerly the Red Cow off-licence.

If you go up Combe Wood Hill, past St Mary's Church, you are rewarded with one of the finest and most extensive views in Essex. It is hard to believe that a big new town is literally only round the corner.

In one of the cottages opposite the thatched cottage known as The Haven in Dry Street lived, in 1890, William Tinworth, the village bootmaker, who had his shop in the small brick annexe. His wife could read and write, an accomplishment at that time, so she wrote and read the letters for the village people.

Well Green Cottages, two red brick buildings at least two hundred years old, stand on the north side of the road at Dry Street between Northlands and Blackman's Farms. Behind the cottages, on a little green, is a well. The water, which is beautifully clear, is still used by the inhabitants of the cottages, although not for drinking. A water cart, drawn by a donkey, used to take the water from this well round the village. It was the only supply and the charge was ½d a pail. About 60 years ago the well was still used, but had been taken over by the local council.

Not far away is the modern Northlands farmhouse. The former timber farmhouse, about 300 years old, stood away from the road, down the hill towards the Stanford bypass. A man was said to have committed suicide there and the bloodstains were to be seen on the floorboards. It was also reputed to be haunted. However securely the latch was fastened on a door in the kitchen it would always open by some invisible agency and there was a most uncanny atmosphere. The house was destroyed by fire in 1933.

Vange County Primary School is the oldest school in the New Town area. The first school was a church school held in the old schoolroom adjoining the cottages standing not far from the entrance to All Saints' Church. The land was given for the erection of these cottages and the school by Sir Charles Smith, lord of the manor and patron of the living in 1858.

A board school of 5 members was formed in 1874 and in 1885 Vange Board School (now the Primary School) was built. In 1886 Miss Roberts was the mistress and there were about 20 children attending.

The records, in copperplate script, date from 1874: they show that the children had a day off to celebrate the Relief of Mafeking in 1900. There are some interesting entries in the log book about the old custom of carrying May garlands round the village. On 1 May, 1893, many of the girls were absent taking flowers round the village and the following 1 May more of the first class girls were absent to 'take round their flowers'. On 2 May, 1898, 'many of the girls were absent carrying round their May garlands'. On 1 May, 1899, 'attendance was only fair'. On 1 May, 1903, many girls were garlanding, but there are no further references after this date. However, in 1916 and 1917 Class III danced round the Maypole on 1 May.

The garlands were two hoops arranged one inside the other and decorated with ribbons and flowers. These were displayed to the villagers and the girls were given a copper or two.

There are also entries relating to children taking dinners to their fathers in the brickfields on the marshes. In 1919 a Juno lamp of 100 candle power was received.

Vange Primary School early this century

Pretoria Lodge, High Road, Vange, c.1950

In 1958 two of the old timber cottages in Vange disappeared. Woodbine Cottages, High Road, were about 120 years old. Although farm labourers last century had large families, their cottages usually only had two bedrooms or one bedroom and a lean-to.

Some years ago there were found in the chimney of the old black cottage with a corrugated iron roof at the bottom of Paynters Hill, Vange, chains on which once hung a kettle or cooking ot over the open fire. This cottage probably once had a thatched roof: its plan is primitive. The two bedrooms open on to an open platform or landing under the lean-to.

At the top of Paynters Hill are still a few timber cottages that once comprised Vange village. That with the hipped tiled roof at the top of the hill was built in the early 19th century with timber from the ancient Vange rectory that stood near the church.

The tiny staircases with latched doors are beside the central chimney, but in the west end is a hatchway in the ceiling through which the inhabitants used to climb by ladder to the upper room.

Near Vange church stand the picturesque red brick Rectory Cottages. Here lived the mistress of the church school. The one-storey building at the eastern end was the first school in Vange, in existence by 1875. In 1886 Miss Roberts was in charge and there were about 20 children.

Ash Cottages, High Road, Pitsea, are typical of the 19th century dwellings of this era. On Gun Hill, Bowers Gifford, there stood by the side of Basildon Bridge (Gale's Corner) a quaint 300 year old cottage.

Langdon Hills Hall, 1963

The patent boots had been bought, the wedding breakfast prepared, the wedding dress made and the licence obtained when Samuel Thistlewood jilted Elizabeth Knight of Langdon Hills. Elizabeth sued her fickle suitor, the case being heard at the Guildhall on 1 February, 1861.

Elizabeth, who was 22 years old, lived with her parents at Langdon Hills Hall, standing near the old church. Her father had answered Samuel's advertisement in *The Times* requiring apartments in the country, with the result that Samuel came from London to live at the Hall. Soon he formed an attachment to Elizabeth and, after due enquiries as to his position in life, was accepted as her suitor, the wedding being fixed for 26 April, 1860. Samuel was 'a gentleman of independent means, having an income of £400 to £500 a year'.

In one letter to Elizabeth he wrote: "Love shall bloom when summer dies," but in another he asked if her father would give her £200. Samuel's education appears to have been somewhat neglected for, in a further letter, he referred to meeting her father at Fenchurch Street when he thought his proposition unreasonable to pay '80 lbs' down and '15 lbs' towards the rent for ten years.

Everything was prepared for the wedding when there came a letter causing the prospective bride to fall on the floor and become 'greatly agitated'. Samuel complained that the captain had been invited to stay for a few days at the hall, but his brother and his wife must go to an inn and be put to expense. They considered themselves grossly insulted and they did not mean to come to the wedding. "I don't think you mean any good towards me in the way you have acted, only for the sake of gain, therefore I shall decline coming also."

The Captain Simmonds referred to in the letter was a man of 70 and not a person of whom Samuel could reasonably be jealous.

Elizabeth did not recover from the shock to her nervous system and, although it was pleaded that Samuel was a man of weak intellect not suited for married life, the jury awarded her £600 damages.

Dunton Hall, with St Mary's in the background. October, 1957

Part of Dunton parish is included in Basildon, but just outside the boundary stood the little church of St Mary, forming part of a picturesque and compact group of church, manor house and farm buildings. By the church entrance was a pond and backing on to the churchyard is the manor house of Dunton Hall.

The church was rebuilt in 1873 at a cost of £1,599, which was raised by subscription. There are, however, still existing several interesting features from the older church on the site. Massive timbers cut from trees that grew 500 years ago support the bell turret and some of the chancel roof timbers are also ancient. Part of the north chancel wall is of 16th century brick.

In the sanctuary stood a carved chair that was in use 200 years ago. There were once two bells, but only the 1712 bell survived until the church became redundant in 1983.

In the porch was a relic of an inhabitant of seven centuries ago; the remains of a heavy stone coffin with shaped headpieces. Whoever was buried in it must have been someone of note. It may have originally been buried in the church floor with the lid forming part of the pavement.

The former Rectory, now a Country Club, was originally moated and St Mary's has become a private residence.

A walk along High Road Pitsea at the end of the 19th century would have shown a parish very little changed in over 800 years. The parish boundary crossed the road near the Working Men's Club and from here there were fields both sides, the road being shaded by wych elms. There was no railway bridge, as the line was not built until 1888.

The first house on the left was Brickhouse Farm, near the site of the Telephone Exchange; on the right was the old Parsonage and then a timber house with wooden shutters to its windows and part of a moat remaining. From here the road wound between fields and elm trees until it reached the site of the Railway Hotel, where stood an old barn belonging to Bluehouse Farm. On the corner of Northlands Drive, then a lane leading to Northlands Farm, stood two timber cottages. Further on was the Railway Tavern.

A wheelwright's stood on what is now the right hand corner of Rectory Park Drive. The next four buildings were the timber house opposite Cook's Stores, two cottages and a blacksmith's. On the right hand corner of Rectory Road was a pond.

Where H J Cook's Store stands was a row of timber cottages, known as Bedlam Row, and then came two timber houses, dated 1721, said to have once been a farmhouse. Next was a wheelwright's and the baker's at the old house with 1641 on its front.

On this side of the road the parish boundary ran through Bluehouse Farm, only the kitchen of the house was in Pitsea. The initials, T S, on the front stood for Thomas Spitty who refronted it in 1806.

The photograph is of Starling's Grocery Store, High Road, Pitsea. After leaving Station Lane there was a field - now the site of a car park and new road - then the beginning of a path over Church Hill and Starling's. Mr Starling is standing in the doorway 80 years ago. Church Path is to the right of the picture.

All these homes have been demolished in the past thirty years.

The everyday lives of the people who lived in Basildon in the 1890s were very far removed from present-day conditions and tales handed down from those days are often amusing. Small events made exciting news, "Have yer heerd the news?" they would say in Vange, "Tatham's brook loose agen." Tatham, bad lad of the village, every now and then caused comment by getting well and truly drunk and going on the rampage.

The roads were so quiet that the young lady organist of Pitsea Church, who lived at Blue House Farm was not worried one Sunday when she found that the farm flock of geese had decided to follow her to church. She had no time to drive them back, so she continued on her way with the geese behind her. They waited outside the church until service ended and then followed her home.

When Thomas Spitty restored and practically rebuilt Blue House, the story is that when he showed his bride round she asked where was the kitchen and it was found that it had been forgotten, so they had to build one on the side: it was in Pitsea Parish, the rest of the farm being in Bowers Gifford.

Basildon people did not like change. Billy Marshall, at the age of 99, when asked at an interview if he liked a glass of beer replied that he had no time 'for they new-fangled things, give me a pot every time'.

Some of the villagers liked a fight. Dick Wife fought Henry Warren from Vange Wharf for a pint of 'pig wittles': Dick won.

At Frierns Farm (The Jolly Friar is near its site) the eccentric owner was jilted on his wedding eve and for many years kept the table set for the wedding breakfast.

The really daring people were the farmer and his family from Hall Farm, Langdon Hills, who, in June 1890, went up in Captain Gale's balloon after it had landed near Langdon Hills old church after ascending from the Crystal Palace.

Eighty years ago Vange was in the depths of the country. A teacher at Vange Primary School (then Vange Board School), near All Saints' Church, recalled how quiet the road was with only the occasional horse and cart passing by.

Children who lived too far away to go home in the winter dinner hours often asked to put scrubbed potatoes under the grate of the classroom fire, so that they were baked ready for the midday break. Children who did not go home were allowed to sit by the fire to eat their sandwiches.

One teacher's home was in a farm building that had been converted into a house on Luncies Farm. Luncies was one of the first farms to be sold for building. Luncies Road is the old farm road.

Vange High Road was very different in those days. Where the huge round-about is in front of the Five Bells was a large field called Crouchmans or Bell Field. There were two small cottages near the fields, then Rectory Cottage and the Rectory with its barn opposite. Next came the school, Vange Hall Cottages with a shop (built in 1883) and Mountfitchet Farm.

Mountfitchet Farm, High Road, Vange, 1932

At the bottom of Paynters Hill were three cottages and here the road turned sharply and steeply up the hill, turning again to where there were the few cottages, all there was of the original village. The tiny one-storey cottage and the old place known as The Cottage, built of timbers from the old Rectory remain, but a quaint thatched dwelling, another cottage and two semidetached timber houses, one of which was formerly the only shop in Vange as well as being the Post Office, have gone.

Near Wharf Road, now built over, were two old blacktarred timber cottages, then came the Barge Inn, Shonks Farm on the right (Bedwell's shop), two little dwellings known as Woodbine Cottages, then only fields until the Pitsea boundary.

The old farmhouse harboured rats and 'meece', as the old folks called them. The farmer's son at Merricks Farm woke up one morning to see his socks moving along the floor - a rat was carrying them away!

The forge, Dunton Road, Laindon, 1912

A former inhabitant of Pitsea had interesting memories of the village at the turn of the century when it was only a few houses on the main road between the church on the little hill and the mill on a rise beyond Beckney Mead (now Howard Park).

Then White House, opposite the park, contained the one and only grocer's shop and was also the bakery, kept by Mr and Mrs Wilsmer. Their two sons were bakers, one going out by horse and cart as far away as Runwell and Rettendon, often getting home after 10 o'clock. Another old inhabitant told me that in 1883 in the deep snow of that year, when Rectory Road had to be cleared of drifts before the traffic could get through, he had to walk from Wickford one night with his horse and cart, kicking his way through the snow, his coat covered with icicles.

In the shop with its little bow window and beamed ceiling groceries and old-fashioned cottage loaves were sold. On the counter stood a box containing packets of Epsom Salts. On the box lid was the verse: 'Here lie I and my four daughters, All through drinking Harrogate waters: Had we but kept to Epsom Salts, We wouldn't be lying in these 'ere vaults'.

There were also local remedies. Mr Reddington, who kept the Post Office and general shop at Bowers Gifford, used to make liniments that 'certainly did cure cuts and bruises'. He sold it in pint bottles and it smelt of turpentine, thyme and beer.

On the north of High Road was the blacksmith's shop, later converted into a bungalow and later still into a shop known as 'The Gables'. It was demolished in the early 1960s. The owner of the bungalow used to have a minister of the Peculiar People come to stay the night and in the morning Mr Crookes of the Bull Inn would drive them to their chapel in Hadleigh.

In the last century Pitsea folk still used the old Essex dialect. They talked of getting 'dreening wet' or of finding hodmedods, which were snails, and if they had a tickling cough they 'tisicked'.

Bowers Gifford Post Office, 1950

Eighty years ago Fobbing Farm, now St Luke's Hospice, was lonely in the fields – now it overlooks Cherrydown and Lee Chapel. It is at the extreme end of Fobbing, which is a very long parish and as it is about 2½ miles from the village the farmer and his family used to attend Vange church, which is nearer.

The farm house is getting on for two hundred years old and was built for the landowner's sister as a private residence. A former farmer's daughter had many happy memories of Fobbing Farm. She recalled the two cellars being good for storing food in hot weather in the days when there were no refrigerators. In one cellar casks of homemade wine were kept. They used to make elderberry wine, the berries being boiled in a large old-fashioned copper in the scullery and on Christmas Eve the wine was tapped and they all drank hot elderberry wine and went to bed feeling on top of the world.

Fobbing Farm was chiefly a corn growing farm and at harvest time, when the corn ripened quickly, a gang of gypsies was employed to help out with the harvesting. They arrived with caravans, horses, and children to camp in a small meadow. Then the fun began. Some casks of beer were stored in the large barn. The first day not much work was done, their attention being focussed on the beer, but after that they worked extremely well. Lusty fellows with powerful muscles, they scythed the corn down and soon made short work of the harvest. All the corn was cut by hand at that time. They had, however, a few playful habits, such as helping themselves to a field of potatoes and tucking in to the tops afterwards as a camouflage: rabbits were regarded as their 'perks'.

The farmer used to speak of a great occasion, the tithe paying dinner held at Basildon Rectory (that used to be in Rectory Road). He used to go to pay tithe for his father's farm in Basildon, Barstable Hall, which stood on the town centre site – which was a very lonely spot.

Charles and Fanny Moss and daughters Georgina and Lily. Photograph by F & E Stoneham, 79 Cheapside, London E.C.

Some Essex policemen of the 1890s

In 1840 the County Police took the place of the unpaid parish constable. Probably the last parish constable of Bowers Gifford was Charles Henry Ellison, the blacksmith who afterwards kept the Gun Inn. One of his daughters, the late Mrs Upson of Bull Farm, Pitsea, could remember when Pitsea did not have a policeman. "We got on very well without one," she said.

The first Pitsea policeman was named Gates and it was he who was scared by a ghost that proved to be a donkey in Pound Lane, Bowers Gifford. In the 1890s the Pitsea policeman lived in Sycamore Cottage, standing on the corner of Rectory Road. His daughter told how, when Pitsea Windmill caught fire, he was on duty at Vange and he ran all the way back to Pitsea. He was so out of breath that he had to lie on the floor to recover.

Then there was no police force other than the Pitsea man in the Basildon area, the nearest other constabulary were at Fobbing, Wickford, Stanford-le-Hope and Billericay, where John Lennon was sergeant with one constable.

By 1910 Vange had a police sergeant, living in High Road, and Bowers Gifford had a constable, living on Gun Hill.

In 1962 a former resident recalled memories of Basildon sixty years previously, when it was an isolated village of scattered houses and farms. She remembered talking to an old lady whose uncle had been parish clerk and master of the little school held in the Priest's house, which was also his home, at the west end of St Nicholas' Church, Laindon. His pupils were mostly the local farmers' sons. He had had three wives, all of whom were buried under the window of the Priest's house.

The older people at this time, she said, firmly believed that Basildon had once been a town and had Roman connections.

Clay Hill was then a lonely country road, quite a creepy place when the mists rose from the damp spots. There was so little traffic that it was quite safe for the ducks to lead their broods across the road to the pond opposite. One dark night a lady fell over a recumbent horse in Wharf Lane, Vange.

The post came from Billericay, the postman walking both ways. He would also oblige by taking boots and shoes back to Billericay for repair. There was no delivery of newspapers and during the time of the Boer War so her grandfather used to ride into Billericay for them. There were no buses until after the Great War.

However, they were not without entertainment. A Southend paper of April, 1912, reported that a concert had been held at Pitsea Congregational Church, and a sketch entitled 'The Pitsea Parish Council' caused much amusement. Vange had a social club that had just held its fourth ball at Fair View Hall, when over a hundred people were present.

The rail fare to Southend was 10d return and a visitor from Basildon for Easter, 1912, could enjoy a programme at a kinema there for 3d or 6d or a visit to the theatre would cost from 4d to 2s.6d.

Clay Hill Road, Basildon, 1931

The agricultural depression of the late 19th century led to many farms in the Basildon area being sold for building. Speculators bought farms, divided them into plots, then to re-sell and make a quick profit.

The company selling land at Vange and Pitsea gave free lunches at the sales held frequently between 1901 and 1906, which were very popular, probably on account of the free liquor. Some sales were difficult to complete as the purchasers got drunk in the sale marquees and, on the way home, tore up their contracts, throwing the pieces out of the train windows, for they had only paid a small deposit. Others bought cheap plots and forgot about them. The sale particulars stated that free tickets for Pitsea were issued any day.

Plots on the elegantly named Alexander Park Estate (up Northlands Drive), 20 ft x 250 ft, cost £8: a half acre was £30 and an acre £50. Plots 20 ft x 120 ft on the Brightside Estate, with frontage to London Road from Howard Park to the Bull Inn cost £35. On the Highlands Estate, Vange, stated to be 150 ft above sea level, plots 20 ft x 100 ft sold for as little as £5.

A sale of plots on River View Estate (formerly Shonks Farm from Merricks Lane to the Working Men's Club) was held on 9 October, 1907, in a marquee near the Barge Inn at 2 p.m. Prices were from £8 for a 20 x 120 ft plot. A 10% deposit was required when signing the contract and immediate possession was given. The balance was payable by 16 quarterly payments if desired.

'Capital roads' said the catalogue, but most plots were some distance from them. Roads were 'formed free', but they were entirely unmade, becoming quagmires in winter. A few false sewer inspection chambers were put in some roads, but there was no hope of sanitation.

The photograph shows a typical asbestos bungalow in Vange in the 1930s. It had 2 bedrooms, one with fireplace; sitting room; and kitchen with sink (although the waste water had to be collected in a pail). There is outdoor sanitation, which can be seen at the side.

When Sir Joseph and Lady Dimsdale arrived at Laindon in 1902 the horses were taken out of the carriage shafts and the men of the village with white ropes pulled it from the Station to their home, Goldsmiths, Langdon Hills.

Sir Joseph was made Lord Mayor of London in November, 1901, and, during his period of office, invited all the Langdon Hills schoolchildren to the Mansion House for the Coronation Procession of King Edward VII and Queen Alexandra on 27 June, 1902. There was also an invitation for the Royal Progress of their Majesties through the City of London on 25 October, 1902, and to a lunch at the Mansion House. Sir Joseph presented each child on leaving with a silver medal in a red morocco case, inscribed on the outside in gold lettering 'Mansion House, Coronation Year, 1902. Right Hon. Sir J.C.Dimsdale, Bart., M.P., Lord Mayor.' The medal has the King on one side and the Queen on the reverse. A former Langdon Hills resident has an invitation for an At Home given by the Dimsdales at Goldsmiths on 16 September, 1902.

A description of Goldsmiths at this time says that the house was comfortable and 'liveable', decorated with taste and judgement and full of interesting things. In the drawingroom, with its antique cabinets and varied collection of rare china, attention was particularly attracted by one novel effect, in the form of a small oblong window inserted in the high white overmantel, giving a charming glimpse, like a 'living picture' of green leaves and waving branches without. There was a collection of state documents, other historic manuscripts and autographed letters of monarchs, soldiers and statesmen.

The Dimsdales were connected with the Society of Friends, although Sir Joseph was a churchman. In 1901 he was 52 years old and had a son in business in India and two daughters, one 'a merry little maiden not yet in her teens' and the elder 'a beautiful young wife'. After his death tragedy struck the family. His son shot himself in a seacoast churchyard and, later, his daughter-in-law died in tragic circumstances in London.

Sir Joseph Dimsdale, M.P.   By permission of the Guildhall Library, London

It was not until this century that the inhabitants of Basildon had the beginnings of amenities. Each village usually had only one small general shop. If you had a well, you were lucky, if not, water had to be brought from a distance, other supplies being from ponds and rainwater butts. A closet (with a pit cleaned out every year or so) at the end of the gardens of both farm and cottage was the only form of sanitation.

Women often helped with the big Monday morning wash at a nearby farm for a small payment, taking younger children with them. In August and September the industrious gleaned in the fields, the corn thus gained being ground at Pitsea Mill, the resultant flour being used for bread making. In the old farmhouse at Gouldings, Vange, there was always a sack of flour obtained by gleaning by a farm worker's wife who lived there.

Some women got tired of it all and ran away. An 1815 advertisement is headed 'Absconded' and gives notice that William Hills, a Laindon shopkeeper would not be responsible for any debts that his wife, Judith, might contract.

A servant at Merricks Farm, Vange, late in the last century, ran away at dawn to Fobbing – taking with her a batch of small pies.

One woman who lived many years ago in a little thatched cottage on High Road, Vange, used to lose her temper occasionally, "I'll leave," she would declare and start to run across the field at the back of the cottage. It was usual for her husband to say to their son as they went after her, "Just catch a hoad on her, Ben," and the woman always returned.

Some of the Moss family who farmed Merricks. John, Ethel, Nella and Leonard, children of Alfred John Moss. 1905

'Populous, prosperous, picturesque Pitsea', glowed a sale catalogue of building plots in 1907. 'Pitsea may become a suburb for those who may have to go to London every day. It is within the zone of projected electric railways and as the distance is so trifling in these days of improving locomotion it may not be long before express trains will accomplish this journey in about 35 minutes.'

There were 19 trains (from 5.22 a.m. to 9.44 p.m.) a day to London, the return fare being 3s.6d. [17½p]. A visit to Southend cost 10d return and a season ticket to Southend was £3.15s.0d. quarterly.

As regards jobs, the nearby 'important and extensive works of Kynochs for the manufacture of cordite, gun cotton, etc.' employed about 700 people. There was also the British Explosive Company's factory on Pitsea Marshes within 'an easy walk'.

It was stated that 'a real garden city without the aid of philanthropists and on a perfectly sound basis is likely to be created'. Land was exceedingly cheap and workers would be able to have large gardens of their own and 'to a certain extent the wishes of many philanthropists will be fulfilled. Nationalisation in this part of the country will then become an established fact'.

It was said to be one of the healthiest localities in England and 'in evidence of the healthiness of Pitsea there is no resident doctor'. In fact, the nearest doctors were in Wickford and Stanford.

The first estate agent in Pitsea. J Ambrose (left) and G Field

Laindon Cinema, opened in 1929

About 70 years ago Vange had a cinema in Central Hall, standing on the left hand corner of Thamesville Drive, opposite the Post Office. It did not last long, although efforts were made to attract patrons: small children were given sticks of rock at the end of performances.

Central Hall was used for concerts and other social events, but, at the time, Fairview Hall in Timberlog Lane was the chief place for dances, concerts, whist drives, etc. This hall stood on the right hand side of Gordon Road and was converted into villas many years ago.

In front of the old Bull Inn in Bull Road, Basildon, stood a long tin shed. This, too, was used for meetings and dances eighty years ago.

In 1846 a draft plan was made for a proposed line of railway from Ilford to Tilbury Fort and Southend with a branch line from Vange to Battlesbridge. The junction would have been at Vange Wharf and the branch line would have run through Luncies Farm, now Luncies Estate, passing through Nevendon to the right of the church.

In the early years of this century farmers living near the railway often used to trespass on the line, using it as a more direct route than the muddy farm lanes to some places, such as the railway station. Two women were carrying their eggs to Pitsea Station and walking on the sleepers deep in conversation. They did not hear an approaching goods train. The driver whistled and they jumped off the line just in time, smashing their eggs in their hurry!

Until the 1914-18 War the population of Basildon had always been small. In 1821 the population was about 1,569 and in 1881 it was 1,457, broken into Basildon 157; Bowers Gifford 197; Laindon 320; Langdon Hills 286; Lee Chapel 12; Nevendon 136; Pitsea 203; and Vange 158. Vange's population increased from 124 in 1821 to 165 in 1831, but Basildon's inhabitants for the same period declined from 142 to 124.

Farming was the chief occupation, but Vange Church registers record the following trades and professions from 1813 - Comptroller of Customs, baker, bargemaster, shopkeeper, shoemaker, brickmaker (1834), publican, organist, butcher, carpenter, railway labourer (1854) gardener and mariner.

A Pitsea Marshes factory built some time before 1906 by Nobels Explosives, Ltd., for the manufacture of cordite was the first factory in the district. An explosion occurred there in the Great War.

New houses were a rarity. When a small house and shop (Westfield's Sweet Shop) were built opposite the entrance to Vange Wharf or Merrick's Lane, Vange, early this century it caused quite a stir.

High Road, Vange, showing Barge Inn, Saunders' Bakery on right and house formerly Westfield's sweet shop

16th century barn, Merricks Farm, Vange. Drawn by Jessie Kestel Payne

Vange Wharf or Merricks Farm was called Bigwoods in the 17th century. The house went back to Tudor times, with old oak ceiling beams. In 1637 the Vange rector, George Maule, wrote of 'being with Thomas Eve in his house called Bigwoods in the hall by the fire' when churchyard fences were discussed.

A map made from a sketch from the hilly fields of the farm shows the property as it was in 1754 when it belonged to Charles Smith of Croydon and comprised 166 acres. Barn Field ran from the large 16th century barn up to the main road. Woodfield Road is now built on part of it, while in 1900 it was a brickfield. The ancient barn simply fell down one summer Sunday afternoon some fifty years ago: Old Tom, a thatcher, who was inside it had a miraculous escape. He had been living in part of the barn and although considerably shaken, his main worry was if the pig's head he had ready to cook could be salvaged from the ruins. It was and the farmer's wife prepared it for him!

A field and marsh called by the curious name 'Merriwigs' formerly belonged to Merricks, although divided from it by Gouldings Farm. It is said that the biggest house in Vange once stood on Merriwigs Marsh and a Merriwigs Farm is mentioned in the church registers of 1602. Merriwigs is probably a corruption of Merricks - in its turn associated with John Meryk of 1515. Merriwigs Field was once known as Kitchen Field and probably grew the food for the house. Probably the house decayed and the land was added to Bigwoods, which then also took that name.

Later known as Riverside Farm it was destroyed by vandals and the whole site is now a timber yard.

GENERAL INDEX

BIOGRAPHICAL INDEX